The Powerful Book of

"I Am" Affirmations

*An Inspirational, Empowering & Positive
Script of Self Affirmations for Attracting
Happiness & Success*

The Self-Affirmation Script

Kiera Zinn

Contents

ISBN-13: 978-1724986689

What is an Affirmation?

An affirmation is a conscious control of your thoughts through short, powerful statements. These thoughts will become your reality. Affirmations are conscious thoughts, they make subconscious become conscious. When you start thinking of positive conscious thoughts, you are also becoming aware of negative thoughts as well.

As human beings, we have 45,000 to 51,000 thoughts a day, that's around 150 to 300 a minute and 80% of those thoughts are negative. Affirmations will change that, statements of assertion declared firmly and with confidence.

So, remember this-

- Today is a new day
- Today is the day you realise your potential
- Today is the day you learn the secrets of life
- Today is the day you will become aware and focus on attracting what you want from life.
- Today is the beginning on the path to change
- You are ready consciously
- You are ready for creating your life experiences
- You are today

How to use Affirmations

It's time to utilise affirmations to remove yourself from a negative mindset and empower yourself.

Positive affirmations WILL help you achieve your dreams and goals in life. If we do repetitive exercises for our body to improve our health then why not use positive mental repetitions for our mind too.

Evidence suggests that by using affirmations you perform better at work. Taking a moment to remind yourself of your best qualities before an important meeting or interview can help calm your nerves, enable a confidence boost and thus improve your chances of the situation.

Affirmations are used to treat people with low self-esteem, depression and other mental health conditions. They have been shown to help stimulate certain areas of our brains to encourage positive changes in our health.

You can use affirmations in any situation in life such as –

- Overcome a bad Habit
- Improve productivity
- Raise confidence
- Improve self-esteem

- Setting goals

Writing affirmations can give you a focus on specific problems in life. Think about what in your life you want to change? Think about whether you would want a more productive day? Do you wish to have a better relationship with friends or family?

Understand that your affirmations should be achievable and credible, For example, if you are stressed about your level of pay, by using positive affirmations as reinforcement, you will raise your confidence to ask for a pay rise.

As an exercise, write down your affirmation, preferably in the present tense. Speak it out loud as if it's already happening, helping you believe that the statement is true. Say it with passion, making it more effective and giving it emotional weight.

Your affirmations should be tailored towards what you want most out of life, common affirmations people use include-

- I love life
- I am confident in my abilities
- I can do this
- I enjoy working with my team
- I'm grateful for my job and how far I've come.

Famous people who use Affirmations

You probably didn't even realise that many famous people use affirmations daily in their lives. They have used positive statements as mantras to further reinforce their belief in themselves. They understand that self-doubt is one of the biggest obstacles in their ability and yet maintain their affirmations to overcome it.

- Arnold Schwarzenegger uses Affirmations, he says that it's the same process that he uses for bodybuilding, and you have to live your life in how you visualize it.
- Denzel Washington utilises affirmations daily, he suggests that you attract not only what you fear but also what you feel and what you are.
- Jim Carrey used to visualize having directors interested in him, he once wrote himself a check for $10,000,000 and dated it Thanksgiving 1995. He put it in his wallet and kept it there for 3 years and just before Thanksgiving 1995, he found out he was going to make $10,000,000 on Dumb and Dumber.
- Lady Gaga repeated to herself "music is my life,

music is my life, and the fame is inside of me." She said that when an affirmation hasn't manifested, it's a lie but you tell yourself over and over and eventually, it becomes true.

- Oprah Winfrey, one of the wealthiest women in the world, famous for going from rags to riches, states that you become what you believe and used affirmations during times of hardship.

- Steve Harvey considers the law of attraction the most powerful book outside of the bible. Like attracts like, you are like a magnet, if you are positive you will draw positive. If you are a kind person, more people are kind to you.

- Will Smith is adamant about the power of Affirmations, He believes that when we dream something and picture it, we commit ourselves to making it a physical reality by putting it into the universe.

Affirmations

The greatest discovery of OUR generation is how, as human beings, we can alter our lives by altering our attitudes of mind.

Ask, believe, receive.

Today is a new day, remember that you are in control of your life and everything you ever wanted is achievable.

The most important two words to know right now is I am. Just by saying these words, you are already manifesting your conscious thoughts into a reality. You are recognising your life and where you are and this will positive reinforcement will attract positive energy and ultimately, a positive outcome.

Listen to the following affirmations, acknowledge them and feel them, visualise the affirmations and imagine that they ARE the reality, imagine with great confidence and without hesitation.

I am Happy to be alive.

I am content in what I have.

I am satisfied in everything right now.

I am relaxed at this moment in time.

I am joyful for my past successes.

I am cheerful for what I have accomplished.

I am blissful for the opportunities that have made me happy.

I am idyllic.

I am tranquil.

I am serene.

I am composed, I know that great things are coming.

I am gratified, I refuse to lose.

I am determined to succeed.

I am thrilled for what's next to come.

I am ecstatic for the future.

I am elated.

I am overjoyed at what I have done with my life.

I am jubilant.

I am proud of myself and the love I receive from everyone around me.

I am triumphant against failures.

I am winning and I have everything I need in life.

I am glorious, I can feel the light of positivity in me.

I am dominant.

I am prevailing, the past holds no power over me.

I am superb.

I am splendid.

I am fabulous, I feel and look amazing.

I am marvellous.

I am stunning.

I am spectacular.

I am remarkable, there is nobody like me in this world.

I am positive and I will maintain this.

I am optimistic for my dreams and goals to manifest into reality.

I am enthusiastic for every new experience and life goal.

I am open to new experiences.

I am exquisite.

I am attractive, I have both inner and outer beauty.

I am gorgeous.

I am elegant.

I am striking and one in a million.

I am prominent.

I am successful.

I am fruitful.

I am prosperous.

I am rich.

I am thriving knowing that I can achieve anything
that I desire.

I am flourishing with no worries.

I am healthy.

I am vigorous.

I am energetic in my goals and dreams which are now
a reality.

I am animated in taking opportunities.

I am robust.

I am tough and have come a long way.

I am hard-hitting.

I am fortunate for everything in life.

I am lucky.

I am privileged.

I am blessed by the universe and its wisdom.

I am sacred and nothing can stand in my way.

I am revered for my kindness and understanding.

I am outstanding in my abilities.

I am notorious for I bring hope to others.

I am infamous.

I am super.

I am excellent in every aspect of my life.

I am tremendous in my skills and approach towards situations.

I am terrific.

I am uncanny.

I am undefeatable in my cause.

I am ready to receive good fortune in my life.

I am focused and without fear.

I am impressive towards others.

I am strong-willed.

I am courageous in my endeavours.

I am industrious in finding solutions.

I am powerful and in control.

I am great.

I am righteous with a high moral standing.

I am brilliant.

I am fun-loving and bring happiness to everyone I meet.

I am efficient in my skills and abilities.

I am dedicated in helping others.

I am dedicated in motivating others.

I am dedicated in bring hope to others.

I am charismatic.

I am alluring, my uniqueness inspires others.

I am charming to the extent that even strangers love me.

I am interesting, I have a lot to offer.

I am stimulating, others love my company and what I have to say.

I am thought-provoking, my mind is a source of wealth.

I am committed to growth.

I am gregarious.

I am outgoing, I make friends easily.

I am extroverted, nothing can stop me.

I am talkative and I will always listen.

I am fluent in communication with everybody I meet.

I am hardworking with no boundaries.

I am committed to love.

I am boundless and will never become bounded.

I am limitless with all the resources I need.

I am infinite.

I am never-ending.

I am inexhaustible, I refuse to give up.

I am vast.

I am everlasting.

I am loved and I love everyone.

I am untouchable.

I am superior.

I am unbeatable, failure has never stopped me.

I am unchallenged, I conquer challenges with ease and experience.

I am unrestricted, I have everything I need to move forward.

I am unconcealed, I am proud of who I am.

I am unconquerable.

I am unhampered.

I am unhindered, I accept struggles and therefore have the know-how to see past them.

I am treasured.

I am precious.

I am cherished.

I am valued for my commitment towards a better, happier life.

I am respected for I reflect positive vibes.

I am esteemed.

I am beloved.

I am adored because I am special.

I am idolised for my vision is about hope, kindness and love.

I am worshipped.

I am precocious and have the initiative to succeed.

I am gifted in my talents.

I am likeable to everyone.

I am momentous.

I am important.

I am earth-shattering.

I am significant to family and friends.

I am promising, I hold my goals, dreams and ambition in a high regard.

I am innovative in my everyday life.

I am experienced and therefore I can settle any situation.

I am ferocious in getting what I want out of life.

I am exceptional.

I am exceptionally powerful.

I am exceptionally gifted.

I am exceptional in everything I commit myself to.

I am kind to everyone.

I am terrific.

I am Heroic and have the confidence to take risks.

I am daring and not afraid.

I am enlightened, everything will fall into place as I see it.

I am appreciative of my life.

I am advantageous in my life right now.

I am honourable for my humbleness.

I am commendable for showing love.

I am worthy.

I am earnest.

I am sincere in how I communicate to everyone.

I am genuine and I aim to be better than yesterday.

I am unaffected by negative thoughts.

I am unpretentious, the real me is more significant and cannot be replaced.

I am modest in my achievements.

I am realistic about my goals and future and therefore I know they will manifest.

I am truthful as this characteristic strengthens my morals.

I am straightforward.

I am significant and remember my influence over others.

I am lively.

I am buoyant, I will always bounce back with a newfound hope.

I am gallant.

I am chivalrous.

I am loyal to everyone who given me hope and love.

I am noble and true to my word.

I am reliable and I am always there for family and friends.

I am unswerving.

I am unshakable, I won't become unhinged.

I am true, the greatest form that I am.

I am unwavering.

I am untiring in my pursuit of happiness.

I am illustrious.

I am recognised and therefore successful.

I am known and therefore remembered.

I am renowned and therefore special.

I am acknowledged and therefore important.

I am emboldened.

I am heartened for the future.

I am inspired to succeed.

I am uplifted to make my dreams and goals come true.

I am vitalised with a boundless energy.

I am invigorated, I can't be swayed.

I am refreshed, I have a vision.

I am restored.

I am revitalised, failures are a thing of the past.

I am fortified with new positive energy.

I am rejuvenated, I am confident and ready for what is next.

I am revived.

I am talented, my abilities have no limits.

I am willing, I am ready to learn whatever I need to succeed.

I am tenacious.

I am insistent.

I am flexible, I will find ways to fix any problem in life.

I am persistent and I won't give up.

I am universal.

I am meaningful, I protect my hopes and dreams.

I am expressive.

I am communicative.

I am explosive in my desires.

I am established and therefore ready to build on my foundations.

I am entitled, I deserve whatever my heart and mind desires.

I am reputable, People hold me in a high regard.

I am authorized.

I am diligent, I have become a master in finding security within myself.

I am meticulous in developing new ways to better myself.

I am thorough in my abilities.

I am duteous.

I am engaged which allows me to focus.

I am substantial.

I am extensive, I can go beyond in order to get everything I need.

I am unhurried, I am here now in the present.

I am ample.

I am idealistic, my reality is I can accomplish anything.

I am accomplished, I have benefited from seeking a better life.

I am equipped for whatever comes.

I am proficient.

I am perfect and refuse to become someone I am not.

I am compelled.

I am feisty.

I am a go-getter, nothing will hold me back ever again.

I am gutsy, I know right from wrong.

I am spirited and I feel positive energies working in my favour.

I am lively.

I am cunning in resolutions and making tough decisions.

I am astute and this allows me to make my dreams come true.

I am smart, I have learned a great deal and now use those experiences.

I am clever, my positive outlook in life only grants me more fortune.

I am knowing.

I am adroit.

I am dexterous, I can do anything.

I am nimble, I can create anything I want.

I am agile, I have the knowledge to expect the unexpected.

I am adept.

I am deft, my skills have given me unparalleled success.

I am professional in my career and unreplaceable.

I am masterful in my knowledge and therefore desirable.

I am capable of many things, many great things.

I am fervent.

I am vehement.

I am fierce, my passion is like fire inside my body.

I am devoted to everything new.

I am logical in making decisions.

I am rational and have the power of wisdom to move forward.

I am insightful and provide motivation for others.

I am wise, my experiences have shaped my life so that I can see clearly now.

I am bright, I am able to deal with any situation.

I am intelligent, nothing can stop me.

I am witty and can entertain and enlighten anyone.

I am funny and see that the little things in life are just as important.

I am hilarious, I can bring joy to anyone I meet.

I am entertaining and use humour to comfort others in times of need.

I am comical in my ability to maintain conversation.

I am eager to develop new ways to improve my life.

I am keen to discover how I can make my dreams a reality.

I am Happy to be alive.

I am content in what I have.

I am satisfied in everything right now.

I am relaxed at this moment in time.

I am joyful for my past successes.

I am cheerful for what I have accomplished.

I am blissful for the opportunities that have made me happy.

I am idyllic.

I am tranquil.

I am serene.

I am composed, I know that great things are coming.

I am gratified, I refuse to lose.

I am determined to succeed.

I am thrilled for what's next to come.

I am ecstatic for the future.

I am elated.

I am overjoyed at what I have done with my life.

I am jubilant.

I am proud of myself and the love I receive from everyone around me.

I am triumphant against failures.

I am winning and I have everything I need in life.

I am glorious, I can feel the light of positivity in me.

I am dominant.

I am prevailing, the past holds no power over me.

I am superb.

I am splendid.

I am fabulous, I feel and look amazing.

I am marvellous.

I am stunning.

I am spectacular.

I am remarkable, there is nobody like me in this world.

I am positive and I will maintain this.

I am optimistic for my dreams and goals to manifest into reality.

I am enthusiastic for every new experience and life goal.

I am open to new experiences.

I am exquisite.

I am attractive, I have both inner and outer beauty.

I am gorgeous.

I am elegant.

I am striking and one in a million.

I am prominent.

I am successful.

I am fruitful.

I am prosperous.

I am rich.

I am thriving knowing that I can achieve anything that I desire.

I am flourishing with no worries.

I am healthy.

I am vigorous.

I am energetic in my goals and dreams which are now a reality.

I am animated in taking opportunities.

I am robust.

I am tough and have come a long way.

I am hard-hitting.

I am fortunate for everything in life.

I am lucky.

I am privileged.

I am blessed by the universe and its wisdom.

I am sacred and nothing can stand in my way.

I am revered for my kindness and understanding.

I am outstanding in my abilities.

I am notorious for I bring hope to others.

I am infamous.

I am super.

I am excellent in every aspect of my life.

I am tremendous in my skills and approach towards situations.

I am terrific.

I am uncanny.

I am undefeatable in my cause.

I am ready to receive good fortune in my life.

I am focused and without fear.

I am impressive towards others.

I am strong-willed.

I am courageous in my endeavours.

I am industrious in finding solutions.

I am powerful and in control.

I am great.

I am righteous with a high moral standing.

I am brilliant.

I am fun-loving and bring happiness to everyone I meet.

I am efficient in my skills and abilities.

I am dedicated in helping others.

I am dedicated in motivating others.

I am dedicated in bring hope to others.

I am charismatic.

I am alluring, my uniqueness inspires others.

I am charming to the extent that even strangers love me.

I am interesting, I have a lot to offer.

I am stimulating, others love my company and what I have to say.

I am thought-provoking, my mind is a source of wealth.

I am committed to growth.

I am gregarious.

I am outgoing, I make friends easily.

I am extroverted, nothing can stop me.

I am talkative and I will always listen.

I am fluent in communication with everybody I meet.

I am hardworking with no boundaries.

I am committed to love.

I am boundless and will never become bounded.

I am limitless with all the resources I need.

I am infinite.

I am never-ending.

I am inexhaustible, I refuse to give up.

I am vast.

I am everlasting.

I am loved and I love everyone.

I am untouchable.

I am superior.

I am unbeatable, failure has never stopped me.

I am unchallenged, I conquer challenges with ease and experience.

I am unrestricted, I have everything I need to move forward.

I am unconcealed, I am proud of who I am.

I am unconquerable.

I am unhampered.

I am unhindered, I accept struggles and therefore have the know-how to see past them.

I am treasured.

I am precious.

I am cherished.

I am valued for my commitment towards a better, happier life.

I am respected for I reflect positive vibes.

I am esteemed.

I am beloved.

I am adored because I am special.

I am idolised for my vision is about hope, kindness and love.

I am worshipped.

I am precocious and have the initiative to succeed.

I am gifted in my talents.

I am likeable to everyone.

I am momentous.

I am important.

I am earth-shattering.

I am significant to family and friends.

I am promising, I hold my goals, dreams and ambition in a high regard.

I am innovative in my everyday life.

I am experienced and therefore I can settle any situation.

I am ferocious in getting what I want out of life.

I am exceptional.

I am exceptionally powerful.

I am exceptionally gifted.

I am exceptional in everything I commit myself to.

I am kind to everyone.

I am terrific.

I am Heroic and have the confidence to take risks.

I am daring and not afraid.

I am enlightened, everything will fall into place as I see it.

I am appreciative of my life.

I am advantageous in my life right now.

I am honourable for my humbleness.

I am commendable for showing love.

I am worthy.

I am earnest.

I am sincere in how I communicate to everyone.

I am genuine and I aim to be better than yesterday.

I am unaffected by negative thoughts.

I am unpretentious, the real me is more significant and cannot be replaced.

I am modest in my achievements.

I am realistic about my goals and future and therefore I know they will manifest.

I am truthful as this characteristic strengthens my morals.

I am straightforward.

I am significant and remember my influence over others.

I am lively.

I am buoyant, I will always bounce back with a newfound hope.

I am gallant.

I am chivalrous.

I am loyal to everyone who given me hope and love.

I am noble and true to my word.

I am reliable and I am always there for family and friends.

I am unswerving.

I am unshakable, I won't become unhinged.

I am true, the greatest form that I am.

I am unwavering.

I am untiring in my pursuit of happiness.

I am illustrious.

I am recognised and therefore successful.

I am known and therefore remembered.

I am renowned and therefore special.

I am acknowledged and therefore important.

I am emboldened.

I am heartened for the future.

I am inspired to succeed.

I am uplifted to make my dreams and goals come true.

I am vitalised with a boundless energy.

I am invigorated, I can't be swayed.

I am refreshed, I have a vision.

I am restored.

I am revitalised, failures are a thing of the past.

I am fortified with new positive energy.

I am rejuvenated, I am confident and ready for what is next.

I am revived.

I am talented, my abilities have no limits.

I am willing, I am ready to learn whatever I need to succeed.

I am tenacious.

I am insistent.

I am flexible, I will find ways to fix any problem in life.

I am persistent and I won't give up.

I am universal.

I am meaningful, I protect my hopes and dreams.

I am expressive.

I am communicative.

I am explosive in my desires.

I am established and therefore ready to build on my foundations.

I am entitled, I deserve whatever my heart and mind desires.

I am reputable, People hold me in a high regard.

I am authorized.

I am diligent, I have become a master in finding security within myself.

I am meticulous in developing new ways to better myself.

I am thorough in my abilities.

I am duteous.

I am engaged which allows me to focus.

I am substantial.

I am extensive, I can go beyond in order to get everything I need.

I am unhurried, I am here now in the present.

I am ample.

I am idealistic, my reality is I can accomplish anything.

I am accomplished, I have benefited from seeking a better life.

I am equipped for whatever comes.

I am proficient.

I am perfect and refuse to become someone I am not.

I am compelled.

I am feisty.

I am a go-getter, nothing will hold me back ever again.

I am gutsy, I know right from wrong.

I am spirited and I feel positive energies working in my favour.

I am lively.

I am cunning in resolutions and making tough decisions.

I am astute and this allows me to make my dreams come true.

I am smart, I have learned a great deal and now use those experiences.

I am clever, my positive outlook in life only grants me more fortune.

I am knowing.

I am adroit.

I am dexterous, I can do anything.

I am nimble, I can create anything I want.

I am agile, I have the knowledge to expect the unexpected.

I am adept.

I am deft, my skills have given me unparalleled success.

I am professional in my career and unreplaceable.

I am masterful in my knowledge and therefore desirable.

I am capable of many things, many great things.

I am fervent.

I am vehement.

I am fierce, my passion is like fire inside my body.

I am devoted to everything new.

I am logical in making decisions.

I am rational and have the power of wisdom to move forward.

I am insightful and provide motivation for others.

I am wise, my experiences have shaped my life so that I can see clearly now.

I am bright, I am able to deal with any situation.

I am intelligent, nothing can stop me.

I am witty and can entertain and enlighten anyone.

I am funny and see that the little things in life are just as important.

I am hilarious, I can bring joy to anyone I meet.

I am entertaining and use humour to comfort others in times of need.

I am comical in my ability to maintain conversation.

I am eager to develop new ways to improve my life.

I am keen to discover how I can make my dreams a reality.

I am Happy to be alive.

I am content in what I have.

I am satisfied in everything right now.

I am relaxed at this moment in time.

I am joyful for my past successes.

I am cheerful for what I have accomplished.

I am blissful for the opportunities that have made me happy.

I am idyllic.

I am tranquil.

I am serene.

I am composed, I know that great things are coming.

I am gratified, I refuse to lose.

I am determined to succeed.

I am thrilled for what's next to come.

I am ecstatic for the future.

I am elated.

I am overjoyed at what I have done with my life.

I am jubilant.

I am proud of myself and the love I receive from everyone around me.

I am triumphant against failures.

I am winning and I have everything I need in life.

I am glorious, I can feel the light of positivity in me.

I am dominant.

I am prevailing, the past holds no power over me.

I am superb.

I am splendid.

I am fabulous, I feel and look amazing.

I am marvellous.

I am stunning.

I am spectacular.

I am remarkable, there is nobody like me in this world.

I am positive and I will maintain this.

I am optimistic for my dreams and goals to manifest into reality.

I am enthusiastic for every new experience and life goal.

I am open to new experiences.

I am exquisite.

I am attractive, I have both inner and outer beauty.

I am gorgeous.

I am elegant.

I am striking and one in a million.

I am prominent.

I am successful.

I am fruitful.

I am prosperous.

I am rich.

I am thriving knowing that I can achieve anything that I desire.

I am flourishing with no worries.

I am healthy.

I am vigorous.

I am energetic in my goals and dreams which are now a reality.

I am animated in taking opportunities.

I am robust.

I am tough and have come a long way.

I am hard-hitting.

I am fortunate for everything in life.

I am lucky.

I am privileged.

I am blessed by the universe and its wisdom.

I am sacred and nothing can stand in my way.

I am revered for my kindness and understanding.

I am outstanding in my abilities.

I am notorious for I bring hope to others.

I am infamous.

I am super.

I am excellent in every aspect of my life.

I am tremendous in my skills and approach towards situations.

I am terrific.

I am uncanny.

I am undefeatable in my cause.

I am ready to receive good fortune in my life.

I am focused and without fear.

I am impressive towards others.

I am strong-willed.

I am courageous in my endeavours.

I am industrious in finding solutions.

I am powerful and in control.

I am great.

I am righteous with a high moral standing.

I am brilliant.

I am fun-loving and bring happiness to everyone I meet.

I am efficient in my skills and abilities.

I am dedicated in helping others.

I am dedicated in motivating others.

I am dedicated in bring hope to others.

I am charismatic.

I am alluring, my uniqueness inspires others.

I am charming to the extent that even strangers love me.

I am interesting, I have a lot to offer.

I am stimulating, others love my company and what I have to say.

I am thought-provoking, my mind is a source of wealth.

I am committed to growth.

I am gregarious.

I am outgoing, I make friends easily.

I am extroverted, nothing can stop me.

I am talkative and I will always listen.

I am fluent in communication with everybody I meet.

I am hardworking with no boundaries.

I am committed to love.

I am boundless and will never become bounded.

I am limitless with all the resources I need.

I am infinite.

I am never-ending.

I am inexhaustible, I refuse to give up.

I am vast.

I am everlasting.

I am loved and I love everyone.

I am untouchable.

I am superior.

I am unbeatable, failure has never stopped me.

I am unchallenged, I conquer challenges with ease and experience.

I am unrestricted, I have everything I need to move forward.

I am unconcealed, I am proud of who I am.

I am unconquerable.

I am unhampered.

I am unhindered, I accept struggles and therefore have the know-how to see past them.

I am treasured.

I am precious.

I am cherished.

I am valued for my commitment towards a better, happier life.

I am respected for I reflect positive vibes.

I am esteemed.

I am beloved.

I am adored because I am special.

I am idolised for my vision is about hope, kindness and love.

I am worshipped.

I am precocious and have the initiative to succeed.

I am gifted in my talents.

I am likeable to everyone.

I am momentous.

I am important.

I am earth-shattering.

I am significant to family and friends.

I am promising, I hold my goals, dreams and ambition in a high regard.

I am innovative in my everyday life.

I am experienced and therefore I can settle any situation.

I am ferocious in getting what I want out of life.

I am exceptional.

I am exceptionally powerful.

I am exceptionally gifted.

I am exceptional in everything I commit myself to.

I am kind to everyone.

I am terrific.

I am Heroic and have the confidence to take risks.

I am daring and not afraid.

I am enlightened, everything will fall into place as I see it.

I am appreciative of my life.

I am advantageous in my life right now.

I am honourable for my humbleness.

I am commendable for showing love.

I am worthy.

I am earnest.

I am sincere in how I communicate to everyone.

I am genuine and I aim to be better than yesterday.

I am unaffected by negative thoughts.

I am unpretentious, the real me is more significant and cannot be replaced.

I am modest in my achievements.

I am realistic about my goals and future and therefore I know they will manifest.

I am truthful as this characteristic strengthens my morals.

I am straightforward.

I am significant and remember my influence over others.

I am lively.

I am buoyant, I will always bounce back with a newfound hope.

I am gallant.

I am chivalrous.

I am loyal to everyone who given me hope and love.

I am noble and true to my word.

I am reliable and I am always there for family and friends.

I am unswerving.

I am unshakable, I won't become unhinged.

I am true, the greatest form that I am.

I am unwavering.

I am untiring in my pursuit of happiness.

I am illustrious.

I am recognised and therefore successful.

I am known and therefore remembered.

I am renowned and therefore special.

I am acknowledged and therefore important.

I am emboldened.

I am heartened for the future.

I am inspired to succeed.

I am uplifted to make my dreams and goals come true.

I am vitalised with a boundless energy.

I am invigorated, I can't be swayed.

I am refreshed, I have a vision.

I am restored.

I am revitalised, failures are a thing of the past.

I am fortified with new positive energy.

I am rejuvenated, I am confident and ready for what is next.

I am revived.

I am talented, my abilities have no limits.

I am willing, I am ready to learn whatever I need to succeed.

I am tenacious.

I am insistent.

I am flexible, I will find ways to fix any problem in life.

I am persistent and I won't give up.

I am universal.

I am meaningful, I protect my hopes and dreams.

I am expressive.

I am communicative.

I am explosive in my desires.

I am established and therefore ready to build on my foundations.

I am entitled, I deserve whatever my heart and mind desires.

I am reputable, People hold me in a high regard.

I am authorized.

I am diligent, I have become a master in finding security within myself.

I am meticulous in developing new ways to better myself.

I am thorough in my abilities.

I am duteous.

I am engaged which allows me to focus.

I am substantial.

I am extensive, I can go beyond in order to get everything I need.

I am unhurried, I am here now in the present.

I am ample.

I am idealistic, my reality is I can accomplish anything.

I am accomplished, I have benefited from seeking a better life.

I am equipped for whatever comes.

I am proficient.

I am perfect and refuse to become someone I am not.

I am compelled.

I am feisty.

I am a go-getter, nothing will hold me back ever again.

I am gutsy, I know right from wrong.

I am spirited and I feel positive energies working in my favour.

I am lively.

I am cunning in resolutions and making tough decisions.

I am astute and this allows me to make my dreams come true.

I am smart, I have learned a great deal and now use those experiences.

I am clever, my positive outlook in life only grants me more fortune.

I am knowing.

I am adroit.

I am dexterous, I can do anything.

I am nimble, I can create anything I want.

I am agile, I have the knowledge to expect the unexpected.

I am adept.

I am deft, my skills have given me unparalleled success.

I am professional in my career and unreplaceable.

I am masterful in my knowledge and therefore desirable.

I am capable of many things, many great things.

I am fervent.

I am vehement.

I am fierce, my passion is like fire inside my body.

I am devoted to everything new.

I am logical in making decisions.

I am rational and have the power of wisdom to move forward.

I am insightful and provide motivation for others.

I am wise, my experiences have shaped my life so that I can see clearly now.

I am bright, I am able to deal with any situation.

I am intelligent, nothing can stop me.

I am witty and can entertain and enlighten anyone.

I am funny and see that the little things in life are just as important.

I am hilarious, I can bring joy to anyone I meet.

I am entertaining and use humour to comfort others in times of need.

I am comical in my ability to maintain conversation.

I am eager to develop new ways to improve my life.

I am keen to discover how I can make my dreams a reality.

I am Happy to be alive.

I am content in what I have.

I am satisfied in everything right now.

I am relaxed at this moment in time.

I am joyful for my past successes.

I am cheerful for what I have accomplished.

I am blissful for the opportunities that have made me happy.

I am idyllic.

I am tranquil.

I am serene.

I am composed, I know that great things are coming.

I am gratified, I refuse to lose.

I am determined to succeed.

I am thrilled for what's next to come.

I am ecstatic for the future.

I am elated.

I am overjoyed at what I have done with my life.

I am jubilant.

I am proud of myself and the love I receive from everyone around me.

I am triumphant against failures.

I am winning and I have everything I need in life.

I am glorious, I can feel the light of positivity in me.

I am dominant.

I am prevailing, the past holds no power over me.

I am superb.

I am splendid.

I am fabulous, I feel and look amazing.

I am marvellous.

I am stunning.

I am spectacular.

I am remarkable, there is nobody like me in this world.

I am positive and I will maintain this.

I am optimistic for my dreams and goals to manifest into reality.

I am enthusiastic for every new experience and life goal.

I am open to new experiences.

I am exquisite.

I am attractive, I have both inner and outer beauty.

I am gorgeous.

I am elegant.

I am striking and one in a million.

I am prominent.

I am successful.

I am fruitful.

I am prosperous.

I am rich.

I am thriving knowing that I can achieve anything that I desire.

I am flourishing with no worries.

I am healthy.

I am vigorous.

I am energetic in my goals and dreams which are now a reality.

I am animated in taking opportunities.

I am robust.

I am tough and have come a long way.

I am hard-hitting.

I am fortunate for everything in life.

I am lucky.

I am privileged.

I am blessed by the universe and its wisdom.

I am sacred and nothing can stand in my way.

I am revered for my kindness and understanding.

I am outstanding in my abilities.

I am notorious for I bring hope to others.

I am infamous.

I am super.

I am excellent in every aspect of my life.

I am tremendous in my skills and approach towards situations.

I am terrific.

I am uncanny.

I am undefeatable in my cause.

I am ready to receive good fortune in my life.

I am focused and without fear.

I am impressive towards others.

I am strong-willed.

I am courageous in my endeavours.

I am industrious in finding solutions.

I am powerful and in control.

I am great.

I am righteous with a high moral standing.

I am brilliant.

I am fun-loving and bring happiness to everyone I meet.

I am efficient in my skills and abilities.

I am dedicated in helping others.

I am dedicated in motivating others.

I am dedicated in bring hope to others.

I am charismatic.

I am alluring, my uniqueness inspires others.

I am charming to the extent that even strangers love me.

I am interesting, I have a lot to offer.

I am stimulating, others love my company and what I have to say.

I am thought-provoking, my mind is a source of wealth.

I am committed to growth.

I am gregarious.

I am outgoing, I make friends easily.

I am extroverted, nothing can stop me.

I am talkative and I will always listen.

I am fluent in communication with everybody I meet.

I am hardworking with no boundaries.

I am committed to love.

I am boundless and will never become bounded.

I am limitless with all the resources I need.

I am infinite.

I am never-ending.

I am inexhaustible, I refuse to give up.

I am vast.

I am everlasting.

I am loved and I love everyone.

I am untouchable.

I am superior.

I am unbeatable, failure has never stopped me.

I am unchallenged, I conquer challenges with ease and experience.

I am unrestricted, I have everything I need to move forward.

I am unconcealed, I am proud of who I am.

I am unconquerable.

I am unhampered.

I am unhindered, I accept struggles and therefore have the know-how to see past them.

I am treasured.

I am precious.

I am cherished.

I am valued for my commitment towards a better, happier life.

I am respected for I reflect positive vibes.

I am esteemed.

I am beloved.

I am adored because I am special.

I am idolised for my vision is about hope, kindness and love.

I am worshipped.

I am precocious and have the initiative to succeed.

I am gifted in my talents.

I am likeable to everyone.

I am momentous.

I am important.

I am earth-shattering.

I am significant to family and friends.

I am promising, I hold my goals, dreams and ambition in a high regard.

I am innovative in my everyday life.

I am experienced and therefore I can settle any situation.

I am ferocious in getting what I want out of life.

I am exceptional.

I am exceptionally powerful.

I am exceptionally gifted.

I am exceptional in everything I commit myself to.

I am kind to everyone.

I am terrific.

I am Heroic and have the confidence to take risks.

I am daring and not afraid.

I am enlightened, everything will fall into place as I see it.

I am appreciative of my life.

I am advantageous in my life right now.

I am honourable for my humbleness.

I am commendable for showing love.

I am worthy.

I am earnest.

I am sincere in how I communicate to everyone.

I am genuine and I aim to be better than yesterday.

I am unaffected by negative thoughts.

I am unpretentious, the real me is more significant and cannot be replaced.

I am modest in my achievements.

I am realistic about my goals and future and therefore I know they will manifest.

I am truthful as this characteristic strengthens my morals.

I am straightforward.

I am significant and remember my influence over others.

I am lively.

I am buoyant, I will always bounce back with a newfound hope.

I am gallant.

I am chivalrous.

I am loyal to everyone who given me hope and love.

I am noble and true to my word.

I am reliable and I am always there for family and friends.

I am unswerving.

I am unshakable, I won't become unhinged.

I am true, the greatest form that I am.

I am unwavering.

I am untiring in my pursuit of happiness.

I am illustrious.

I am recognised and therefore successful.

I am known and therefore remembered.

I am renowned and therefore special.

I am acknowledged and therefore important.

I am emboldened.

I am heartened for the future.

I am inspired to succeed.

I am uplifted to make my dreams and goals come true.

I am vitalised with a boundless energy.

I am invigorated, I can't be swayed.

I am refreshed, I have a vision.

I am restored.

I am revitalised, failures are a thing of the past.

I am fortified with new positive energy.

I am rejuvenated, I am confident and ready for what is next.

I am revived.

I am talented, my abilities have no limits.

I am willing, I am ready to learn whatever I need to succeed.

I am tenacious.

I am insistent.

I am flexible, I will find ways to fix any problem in life.

I am persistent and I won't give up.

I am universal.

I am meaningful, I protect my hopes and dreams.

I am expressive.

I am communicative.

I am explosive in my desires.

I am established and therefore ready to build on my foundations.

I am entitled, I deserve whatever my heart and mind desires.

I am reputable, People hold me in a high regard.

I am authorized.

I am diligent, I have become a master in finding security within myself.

I am meticulous in developing new ways to better myself.

I am thorough in my abilities.

I am duteous.

I am engaged which allows me to focus.

I am substantial.

I am extensive, I can go beyond in order to get everything I need.

I am unhurried, I am here now in the present.

I am ample.

I am idealistic, my reality is I can accomplish anything.

I am accomplished, I have benefited from seeking a better life.

I am equipped for whatever comes.

I am proficient.

I am perfect and refuse to become someone I am not.

I am compelled.

I am feisty.

I am a go-getter, nothing will hold me back ever again.

I am gutsy, I know right from wrong.

I am spirited and I feel positive energies working in my favour.

I am lively.

I am cunning in resolutions and making tough decisions.

I am astute and this allows me to make my dreams come true.

I am smart, I have learned a great deal and now use those experiences.

I am clever, my positive outlook in life only grants me more fortune.

I am knowing.

I am adroit.

I am dexterous, I can do anything.

I am nimble, I can create anything I want.

I am agile, I have the knowledge to expect the unexpected.

I am adept.

I am deft, my skills have given me unparalleled success.

I am professional in my career and unreplaceable.

I am masterful in my knowledge and therefore desirable.

I am capable of many things, many great things.

I am fervent.

I am vehement.

I am fierce, my passion is like fire inside my body.

I am devoted to everything new.

I am logical in making decisions.

I am rational and have the power of wisdom to move forward.

I am insightful and provide motivation for others.

I am wise, my experiences have shaped my life so that I can see clearly now.

I am bright, I am able to deal with any situation.

I am intelligent, nothing can stop me.

I am witty and can entertain and enlighten anyone.

I am funny and see that the little things in life are just as important.

I am hilarious, I can bring joy to anyone I meet.

I am entertaining and use humour to comfort others in times of need.

I am comical in my ability to maintain conversation.

I am eager to develop new ways to improve my life.

I am keen to discover how I can make my dreams a reality.

I am Happy to be alive.

I am content in what I have.

I am satisfied in everything right now.

I am relaxed at this moment in time.

I am joyful for my past successes.

I am cheerful for what I have accomplished.

I am blissful for the opportunities that have made me happy.

I am idyllic.

I am tranquil.

I am serene.

I am composed, I know that great things are coming.

I am gratified, I refuse to lose.

I am determined to succeed.

I am thrilled for what's next to come.

I am ecstatic for the future.

I am elated.

I am overjoyed at what I have done with my life.

I am jubilant.

I am proud of myself and the love I receive from everyone around me.

I am triumphant against failures.

I am winning and I have everything I need in life.

I am glorious, I can feel the light of positivity in me.

I am dominant.

I am prevailing, the past holds no power over me.

I am superb.

I am splendid.

I am fabulous, I feel and look amazing.

I am marvellous.

I am stunning.

I am spectacular.

I am remarkable, there is nobody like me in this world.

I am positive and I will maintain this.

I am optimistic for my dreams and goals to manifest into reality.

I am enthusiastic for every new experience and life goal.

I am open to new experiences.

I am exquisite.

I am attractive, I have both inner and outer beauty.

I am gorgeous.

I am elegant.

I am striking and one in a million.

I am prominent.

I am successful.

I am fruitful.

I am prosperous.

I am rich.

I am thriving knowing that I can achieve anything that I desire.

I am flourishing with no worries.

I am healthy.

I am vigorous.

I am energetic in my goals and dreams which are now a reality.

I am animated in taking opportunities.

I am robust.

I am tough and have come a long way.

I am hard-hitting.

I am fortunate for everything in life.

I am lucky.

I am privileged.

I am blessed by the universe and its wisdom.

I am sacred and nothing can stand in my way.

I am revered for my kindness and understanding.

I am outstanding in my abilities.

I am notorious for I bring hope to others.

I am infamous.

I am super.

I am excellent in every aspect of my life.

I am tremendous in my skills and approach towards situations.

I am terrific.

I am uncanny.

I am undefeatable in my cause.

I am ready to receive good fortune in my life.

I am focused and without fear.

I am impressive towards others.

I am strong-willed.

I am courageous in my endeavours.

I am industrious in finding solutions.

I am powerful and in control.

I am great.

I am righteous with a high moral standing.

I am brilliant.

I am fun-loving and bring happiness to everyone I meet.

I am efficient in my skills and abilities.

I am dedicated in helping others.

I am dedicated in motivating others.

I am dedicated in bring hope to others.

I am charismatic.

I am alluring, my uniqueness inspires others.

I am charming to the extent that even strangers love me.

I am interesting, I have a lot to offer.

I am stimulating, others love my company and what I have to say.

I am thought-provoking, my mind is a source of wealth.

I am committed to growth.

I am gregarious.

I am outgoing, I make friends easily.

I am extroverted, nothing can stop me.

I am talkative and I will always listen.

I am fluent in communication with everybody I meet.

I am hardworking with no boundaries.

I am committed to love.

I am boundless and will never become bounded.

I am limitless with all the resources I need.

I am infinite.

I am never-ending.

I am inexhaustible, I refuse to give up.

I am vast.

I am everlasting.

I am loved and I love everyone.

I am untouchable.

I am superior.

I am unbeatable, failure has never stopped me.

I am unchallenged, I conquer challenges with ease and experience.

I am unrestricted, I have everything I need to move forward.

I am unconcealed, I am proud of who I am.

I am unconquerable.

I am unhampered.

I am unhindered, I accept struggles and therefore have the know-how to see past them.

I am treasured.

I am precious.

I am cherished.

I am valued for my commitment towards a better, happier life.

I am respected for I reflect positive vibes.

I am esteemed.

I am beloved.

I am adored because I am special.

I am idolised for my vision is about hope, kindness and love.

I am worshipped.

I am precocious and have the initiative to succeed.

I am gifted in my talents.

I am likeable to everyone.

I am momentous.

I am important.

I am earth-shattering.

I am significant to family and friends.

I am promising, I hold my goals, dreams and ambition in a high regard.

I am innovative in my everyday life.

I am experienced and therefore I can settle any situation.

I am ferocious in getting what I want out of life.

I am exceptional.

I am exceptionally powerful.

I am exceptionally gifted.

I am exceptional in everything I commit myself to.

I am kind to everyone.

I am terrific.

I am Heroic and have the confidence to take risks.

I am daring and not afraid.

I am enlightened, everything will fall into place as I see it.

I am appreciative of my life.

I am advantageous in my life right now.

I am honourable for my humbleness.

I am commendable for showing love.

I am worthy.

I am earnest.

I am sincere in how I communicate to everyone.

I am genuine and I aim to be better than yesterday.

I am unaffected by negative thoughts.

I am unpretentious, the real me is more significant and cannot be replaced.

I am modest in my achievements.

I am realistic about my goals and future and therefore I know they will manifest.

I am truthful as this characteristic strengthens my morals.

I am straightforward.

I am significant and remember my influence over others.

I am lively.

I am buoyant, I will always bounce back with a newfound hope.

I am gallant.

I am chivalrous.

I am loyal to everyone who given me hope and love.

I am noble and true to my word.

I am reliable and I am always there for family and friends.

I am unswerving.

I am unshakable, I won't become unhinged.

I am true, the greatest form that I am.

I am unwavering.

I am untiring in my pursuit of happiness.

I am illustrious.

I am recognised and therefore successful.

I am known and therefore remembered.

I am renowned and therefore special.

I am acknowledged and therefore important.

I am emboldened.

I am heartened for the future.

I am inspired to succeed.

I am uplifted to make my dreams and goals come true.

I am vitalised with a boundless energy.

I am invigorated, I can't be swayed.

I am refreshed, I have a vision.

I am restored.

I am revitalised, failures are a thing of the past.

I am fortified with new positive energy.

I am rejuvenated, I am confident and ready for what is next.

I am revived.

I am talented, my abilities have no limits.

I am willing, I am ready to learn whatever I need to succeed.

I am tenacious.

I am insistent.

I am flexible, I will find ways to fix any problem in life.

I am persistent and I won't give up.

I am universal.

I am meaningful, I protect my hopes and dreams.

I am expressive.

I am communicative.

I am explosive in my desires.

I am established and therefore ready to build on my foundations.

I am entitled, I deserve whatever my heart and mind desires.

I am reputable, People hold me in a high regard.

I am authorized.

I am diligent, I have become a master in finding security within myself.

I am meticulous in developing new ways to better myself.

I am thorough in my abilities.

I am duteous.

I am engaged which allows me to focus.

I am substantial.

I am extensive, I can go beyond in order to get everything I need.

I am unhurried, I am here now in the present.

I am ample.

I am idealistic, my reality is I can accomplish anything.

I am accomplished, I have benefited from seeking a better life.

I am equipped for whatever comes.

I am proficient.

I am perfect and refuse to become someone I am not.

I am compelled.

I am feisty.

I am a go-getter, nothing will hold me back ever again.

I am gutsy, I know right from wrong.

I am spirited and I feel positive energies working in my favour.

I am lively.

I am cunning in resolutions and making tough decisions.

I am astute and this allows me to make my dreams come true.

I am smart, I have learned a great deal and now use those experiences.

I am clever, my positive outlook in life only grants me more fortune.

I am knowing.

I am adroit.

I am dexterous, I can do anything.

I am nimble, I can create anything I want.

I am agile, I have the knowledge to expect the unexpected.

I am adept.

I am deft, my skills have given me unparalleled success.

I am professional in my career and unreplaceable.

I am masterful in my knowledge and therefore desirable.

I am capable of many things, many great things.

I am fervent.

I am vehement.

I am fierce, my passion is like fire inside my body.

I am devoted to everything new.

I am logical in making decisions.

I am rational and have the power of wisdom to move forward.

I am insightful and provide motivation for others.

I am wise, my experiences have shaped my life so that I can see clearly now.

I am bright, I am able to deal with any situation.

I am intelligent, nothing can stop me.

I am witty and can entertain and enlighten anyone.

I am funny and see that the little things in life are just as important.

I am hilarious, I can bring joy to anyone I meet.

I am entertaining and use humour to comfort others in times of need.

I am comical in my ability to maintain conversation.

I am eager to develop new ways to improve my life.

I am keen to discover how I can make my dreams a reality.

I am Happy to be alive.

I am content in what I have.

I am satisfied in everything right now.

I am relaxed at this moment in time.

I am joyful for my past successes.

I am cheerful for what I have accomplished.

I am blissful for the opportunities that have made me happy.

I am idyllic.

I am tranquil.

I am serene.

I am composed, I know that great things are coming.

I am gratified, I refuse to lose.

I am determined to succeed.

I am thrilled for what's next to come.

I am ecstatic for the future.

I am elated.

I am overjoyed at what I have done with my life.

I am jubilant.

I am proud of myself and the love I receive from everyone around me.

I am triumphant against failures.

I am winning and I have everything I need in life.

I am glorious, I can feel the light of positivity in me.

I am dominant.

I am prevailing, the past holds no power over me.

I am superb.

I am splendid.

I am fabulous, I feel and look amazing.

I am marvellous.

I am stunning.

I am spectacular.

I am remarkable, there is nobody like me in this world.

I am positive and I will maintain this.

I am optimistic for my dreams and goals to manifest into reality.

I am enthusiastic for every new experience and life goal.

I am open to new experiences.

I am exquisite.

I am attractive, I have both inner and outer beauty.

I am gorgeous.

I am elegant.

I am striking and one in a million.

I am prominent.

I am successful.

I am fruitful.

I am prosperous.

I am rich.

I am thriving knowing that I can achieve anything that I desire.

I am flourishing with no worries.

I am healthy.

I am vigorous.

I am energetic in my goals and dreams which are now a reality.

I am animated in taking opportunities.

I am robust.

I am tough and have come a long way.

I am hard-hitting.

I am fortunate for everything in life.

I am lucky.

I am privileged.

I am blessed by the universe and its wisdom.

I am sacred and nothing can stand in my way.

I am revered for my kindness and understanding.

I am outstanding in my abilities.

I am notorious for I bring hope to others.

I am infamous.

I am super.

I am excellent in every aspect of my life.

I am tremendous in my skills and approach towards situations.

I am terrific.

I am uncanny.

I am undefeatable in my cause.

I am ready to receive good fortune in my life.

I am focused and without fear.

I am impressive towards others.

I am strong-willed.

I am courageous in my endeavours.

I am industrious in finding solutions.

I am powerful and in control.

I am great.

I am righteous with a high moral standing.

I am brilliant.

I am fun-loving and bring happiness to everyone I meet.

I am efficient in my skills and abilities.

I am dedicated in helping others.

I am dedicated in motivating others.

I am dedicated in bring hope to others.

I am charismatic.

I am alluring, my uniqueness inspires others.

I am charming to the extent that even strangers love me.

I am interesting, I have a lot to offer.

I am stimulating, others love my company and what I have to say.

I am thought-provoking, my mind is a source of wealth.

I am committed to growth.

I am gregarious.

I am outgoing, I make friends easily.

I am extroverted, nothing can stop me.

I am talkative and I will always listen.

I am fluent in communication with everybody I meet.

I am hardworking with no boundaries.

I am committed to love.

I am boundless and will never become bounded.

I am limitless with all the resources I need.

I am infinite.

I am never-ending.

I am inexhaustible, I refuse to give up.

I am vast.

I am everlasting.

I am loved and I love everyone.

I am untouchable.

I am superior.

I am unbeatable, failure has never stopped me.

I am unchallenged, I conquer challenges with ease and experience.

I am unrestricted, I have everything I need to move forward.

I am unconcealed, I am proud of who I am.

I am unconquerable.

I am unhampered.

I am unhindered, I accept struggles and therefore have the know-how to see past them.

I am treasured.

I am precious.

I am cherished.

I am valued for my commitment towards a better, happier life.

I am respected for I reflect positive vibes.

I am esteemed.

I am beloved.

I am adored because I am special.

I am idolised for my vision is about hope, kindness and love.

I am worshipped.

I am precocious and have the initiative to succeed.

I am gifted in my talents.

I am likeable to everyone.

I am momentous.

I am important.

I am earth-shattering.

I am significant to family and friends.

I am promising, I hold my goals, dreams and ambition in a high regard.

I am innovative in my everyday life.

I am experienced and therefore I can settle any situation.

I am ferocious in getting what I want out of life.

I am exceptional.

I am exceptionally powerful.

I am exceptionally gifted.

I am exceptional in everything I commit myself to.

I am kind to everyone.

I am terrific.

I am Heroic and have the confidence to take risks.

I am daring and not afraid.

I am enlightened, everything will fall into place as I see it.

I am appreciative of my life.

I am advantageous in my life right now.

I am honourable for my humbleness.

I am commendable for showing love.

I am worthy.

I am earnest.

I am sincere in how I communicate to everyone.

I am genuine and I aim to be better than yesterday.

I am unaffected by negative thoughts.

I am unpretentious, the real me is more significant and cannot be replaced.

I am modest in my achievements.

I am realistic about my goals and future and therefore I know they will manifest.

I am truthful as this characteristic strengthens my morals.

I am straightforward.

I am significant and remember my influence over others.

I am lively.

I am buoyant, I will always bounce back with a newfound hope.

I am gallant.

I am chivalrous.

I am loyal to everyone who given me hope and love.

I am noble and true to my word.

I am reliable and I am always there for family and friends.

I am unswerving.

I am unshakable, I won't become unhinged.

I am true, the greatest form that I am.

I am unwavering.

I am untiring in my pursuit of happiness.

I am illustrious.

I am recognised and therefore successful.

I am known and therefore remembered.

I am renowned and therefore special.

I am acknowledged and therefore important.

I am emboldened.

I am heartened for the future.

I am inspired to succeed.

I am uplifted to make my dreams and goals come true.

I am vitalised with a boundless energy.

I am invigorated, I can't be swayed.

I am refreshed, I have a vision.

I am restored.

I am revitalised, failures are a thing of the past.

I am fortified with new positive energy.

I am rejuvenated, I am confident and ready for what is next.

I am revived.

I am talented, my abilities have no limits.

I am willing, I am ready to learn whatever I need to succeed.

I am tenacious.

I am insistent.

I am flexible, I will find ways to fix any problem in life.

I am persistent and I won't give up.

I am universal.

I am meaningful, I protect my hopes and dreams.

I am expressive.

I am communicative.

I am explosive in my desires.

I am established and therefore ready to build on my foundations.

I am entitled, I deserve whatever my heart and mind desires.

I am reputable, People hold me in a high regard.

I am authorized.

I am diligent, I have become a master in finding security within myself.

I am meticulous in developing new ways to better myself.

I am thorough in my abilities.

I am duteous.

I am engaged which allows me to focus.

I am substantial.

I am extensive, I can go beyond in order to get everything I need.

I am unhurried, I am here now in the present.

I am ample.

I am idealistic, my reality is I can accomplish anything.

I am accomplished, I have benefited from seeking a better life.

I am equipped for whatever comes.

I am proficient.

I am perfect and refuse to become someone I am not.

I am compelled.

I am feisty.

I am a go-getter, nothing will hold me back ever again.

I am gutsy, I know right from wrong.

I am spirited and I feel positive energies working in my favour.

I am lively.

I am cunning in resolutions and making tough decisions.

I am astute and this allows me to make my dreams come true.

I am smart, I have learned a great deal and now use those experiences.

I am clever, my positive outlook in life only grants me more fortune.

I am knowing.

I am adroit.

I am dexterous, I can do anything.

I am nimble, I can create anything I want.

I am agile, I have the knowledge to expect the unexpected.

I am adept.

I am deft, my skills have given me unparalleled success.

I am professional in my career and unreplaceable.

I am masterful in my knowledge and therefore desirable.

I am capable of many things, many great things.

I am fervent.

I am vehement.

I am fierce, my passion is like fire inside my body.

I am devoted to everything new.

I am logical in making decisions.

I am rational and have the power of wisdom to move forward.

I am insightful and provide motivation for others.

I am wise, my experiences have shaped my life so that I can see clearly now.

I am bright, I am able to deal with any situation.

I am intelligent, nothing can stop me.

I am witty and can entertain and enlighten anyone.

I am funny and see that the little things in life are just as important.

I am hilarious, I can bring joy to anyone I meet.

I am entertaining and use humour to comfort others in times of need.

I am comical in my ability to maintain conversation.

I am eager to develop new ways to improve my life.

I am keen to discover how I can make my dreams a reality.

I am Happy to be alive.

I am content in what I have.

I am satisfied in everything right now.

I am relaxed at this moment in time.

I am joyful for my past successes.

I am cheerful for what I have accomplished.

I am blissful for the opportunities that have made me happy.

I am idyllic.

I am tranquil.

I am serene.

I am composed, I know that great things are coming.

I am gratified, I refuse to lose.

I am determined to succeed.

I am thrilled for what's next to come.

I am ecstatic for the future.

I am elated.

I am overjoyed at what I have done with my life.

I am jubilant.

I am proud of myself and the love I receive from everyone around me.

I am triumphant against failures.

I am winning and I have everything I need in life.

I am glorious, I can feel the light of positivity in me.

I am dominant.

I am prevailing, the past holds no power over me.

I am superb.

I am splendid.

I am fabulous, I feel and look amazing.

I am marvellous.

I am stunning.

I am spectacular.

I am remarkable, there is nobody like me in this world.

I am positive and I will maintain this.

I am optimistic for my dreams and goals to manifest into reality.

I am enthusiastic for every new experience and life goal.

I am open to new experiences.

I am exquisite.

I am attractive, I have both inner and outer beauty.

I am gorgeous.

I am elegant.

I am striking and one in a million.

I am prominent.

I am successful.

I am fruitful.

I am prosperous.

I am rich.

I am thriving knowing that I can achieve anything that I desire.

I am flourishing with no worries.

I am healthy.

I am vigorous.

I am energetic in my goals and dreams which are now a reality.

I am animated in taking opportunities.

I am robust.

I am tough and have come a long way.

I am hard-hitting.

I am fortunate for everything in life.

I am lucky.

I am privileged.

I am blessed by the universe and its wisdom.

I am sacred and nothing can stand in my way.

I am revered for my kindness and understanding.

I am outstanding in my abilities.

I am notorious for I bring hope to others.

I am infamous.

I am super.

I am excellent in every aspect of my life.

I am tremendous in my skills and approach towards situations.

I am terrific.

I am uncanny.

I am undefeatable in my cause.

I am ready to receive good fortune in my life.

I am focused and without fear.

I am impressive towards others.

I am strong-willed.

I am courageous in my endeavours.

I am industrious in finding solutions.

I am powerful and in control.

I am great.

I am righteous with a high moral standing.

I am brilliant.

I am fun-loving and bring happiness to everyone I meet.

I am efficient in my skills and abilities.

I am dedicated in helping others.

I am dedicated in motivating others.

I am dedicated in bring hope to others.

I am charismatic.

I am alluring, my uniqueness inspires others.

I am charming to the extent that even strangers love me.

I am interesting, I have a lot to offer.

I am stimulating, others love my company and what I have to say.

I am thought-provoking, my mind is a source of wealth.

I am committed to growth.

I am gregarious.

I am outgoing, I make friends easily.

I am extroverted, nothing can stop me.

I am talkative and I will always listen.

I am fluent in communication with everybody I meet.

I am hardworking with no boundaries.

I am committed to love.

I am unlimited and will never become bounded.

I am limitless with all the resources I need.

I am infinite.

I am never-ending.

I am bottomless, I refuse to give up.

I am vast.

I am ceaseless.

Made in the USA
Las Vegas, NV
26 February 2022

44632657R00059